In the Water ...
On the Water

By Dorothy Chlad

Illustrations by Lydia Halverson

CHILDRENS PRESS ®

CHICAGO

This book is dedicated to Michael and Kristin Doroshewitz, my two grandchildren, and their mother Tammy and their father Mick—for the happiness they have given to grandma and grandpa.

Safety Town is a comprehensive educational program that introduces safety awareness and preventive procedures to preschool children. During the twenty-hour course, children learn—through their own involvement—safety rules about fire, poison, strangers, traffic, home, train, car, bus, playground, animals, toys, etc. They participate in safety activities in the indoor classroom and practice safety lessons on the outdoor layout, which consists of a miniature town complete with houses, sidewalks, and crosswalks. Role-playing in simulated and real-life situations, under the guidance of a teacher and uniformed personnel, provides children with learning experiences. This allows them to respond properly when confronted with potentially dangerous situations that occur in everyday life.

National Safety Town Center, established in 1964, is the pioneer organization dedicated to promoting preschool-early childhood safety education. This nonprofit organization has been largely responsible for enlightening the media, corporations, government officials, and the general public to the importance of safety education for children. Its network of dedicated volunteers continually supports and promotes the importance of safety for children through the Safety Town program.

For more information about the Safety Town program please contact

National Safety Town Center
P.O. Box 39312
Cleveland, Ohio 44139
216-831-7433

Library of Congress Cataloging-in-Publication Data

Chlad, Dorothy.
   In the water—on the water / by Dorothy Chlad.
        p.   cm. — (Safety Town)
   Summary: Michael and Kristin give pointers on water
safety—at the beach, in the pool, fishing, and in the
bathtub.
   ISBN 0-516-01974-0
   1. Aquatic sports—Safety measures—Juvenile
literature. [1. Aquatic sports—Safety
measures. 2. Safety.] I. Title. II. Series: Chlad,
Dorothy. Safety town.
GV770.6.C45 1988   88-12065
797'.028'9—dc19   CIP
                                      AC

Hi, my name is Michael
and this is my sister Kristin.

We are going to tell you how to have fun and be safe . . . in the water and on the water.

5

When we go to the beach, we play in the sand.

We have fun!

We ALWAYS wear
a life jacket. Sometimes
a big wave pushes
us down.

9

NEVER throw sand.

When sand gets
in your eyes, it hurts.

Sometimes I swim
in my pool with my
friends.

My sister plays
in her pool with
her friends.

Our friend has an indoor pool. Sometimes we swim and play at her house.

We ALWAYS use
the steps and hold
onto the railing when
we go in and out of
the pool.

NEVER jump into a pool.

You could hurt someone.

At a big pool or at the beach, there are lifeguards. They help people and tell us the rules.

When we go fishing, we wear life jackets.

It is fun to fish.
Grandpa helps me.

Sometimes Daddy
goes water-skiing.

He makes big waves
and splashes. That is fun
to watch.

In the bathtub, I play
with my toys.

NEVER play with the
faucets. You could get
burned.

Mom and Dad
love us. They want
us to have fun
and be safe.

29

Please remember
our water rules.

- ALWAYS wear a life jacket

- NEVER throw sand

- NEVER jump into a pool

- ALWAYS use the steps and railing

- NEVER play with faucets

About the Author

Dorothy Chlad, founder of the total concept of Safety Town, is recognized internationally as a leader in Preschool/Early Childhood Safety Education. She has authored eight comprehensive books on the program and has conducted nationally the only workshops dedicated to the concept. Under Mrs. Chlad's direction and leadership, the National Safety Town Center has grown to international stature.

Dorothy Chlad serves as a consultant for State Departments of Safety and Education. She also has consulted for the children's TV programs, Sesame Street and the Jim Henson Muppet Traffic Safety Show.

She lectures extensively and has presented the importance of safety education at such conferences as the National Community Education Association, National Safety Council, World Safety Congress, and the American Driver and Traffic Safety Education Association. She serves on several national committees such as the Highway Traffic Safety Division and the Educational Resources Division of National Safety Council, National Coalition to Prevent Childhood Injuries. Mrs. Chlad, a fellow in the National Academy of Safety Education, sits on the governing board of the International Safety Hall of Fame and is an active participant in numerous safety organizations such as the National Safety Council, Alliance for Traffic Safety, American Society of Safety Engineers, World Safety Organization, American Driver and Traffic Safety Education Association, Veterans of Safety and National Association for Education of Young Children.

A participant of White House Conferences on safety, Dorothy Chlad has received numerous honors and awards including National Volunteer Activist and YMCA Career Woman of Achievement in 1983. She received the **President's Volunteer Action Award** from President Reagan for twenty years of Safety Town efforts, and in 1986, Cedar Crest College in Pennsylvania presented her with an honorary degree, Doctor of Humane Letters. She has been selected for inclusion in **Who's Who of American Women**, **Personalities of America**, the **International Directory of Distinguished Leadership**, and **The World Who's Who of Women.**

About the Artist

Lydia Halverson attended the University of Illinois, graduating with a degree in fine arts. She worked as a graphic designer for many years before finally concentrating on book illustration.

Lydia lives with her husband and two cats in a suburb of Chicago, and is active in several environmental organizations.